FOR ELIZA

MEET INDOMITABLE SPIRIT

INDOMITABLE SPIRIT IS CONFIDENT

INDOMITABLE SPIRIT IS COURAGEOUS

INDOMITABLE SPIRIT IS RESILIENT

INDOMITABLE SPIRIT IS UNSTOPPABLE

WHEN INDOMITABLE SPIRIT IS FEELING NERVOUS OR SCARED

HE STANDS UP IN THE FACE OF FEAR NEVER LETTING IT SHATTER HIS CONFIDENCE OR SELF WORTH

WHEN THE SITUATION JUST DOES NOT SEEM FAIR

INDOMITABLE SPIRIT DOES NOT TAKE THINGS PERSONALLY

AND HE FINDS WAYS TO REMAIN FULFILLED

WHEN INDOMITABLE SPIRIT IS DISCOURAGED

HE REMAINS CALM

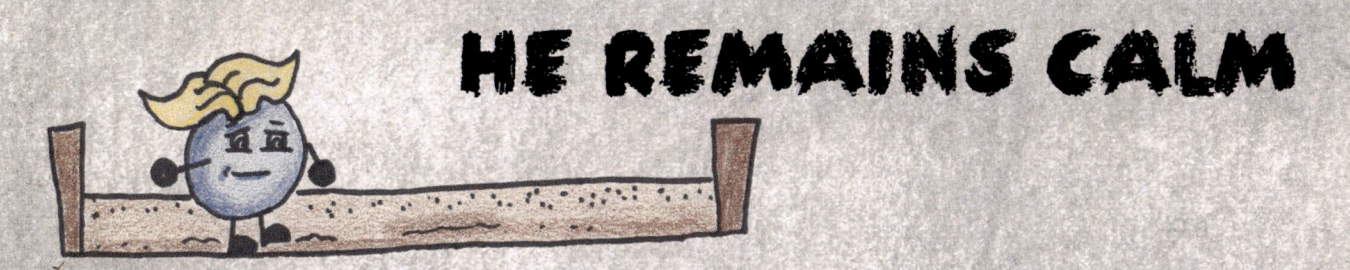

AND SEES EVERY FAILURE

AS A STEP TOWARDS SUCCESS

WHEN INDOMITABLE SPIRIT FEELS BACKED INTO A CORNER

HE ALWAYS FINDS A WAY TO MAKE IT OUT ALRIGHT

WHEN INDOMITABLE SPIRIT IS BEING ATTACKED BY HURTFUL OR OPPRESSIVE WORDS

HE NEVER TAKES THE WORDS TO HEART

AND WHEN THOSE WORDS COME BACK INTO HIS MEMORY

HE REFUTES THEM BEFORE THEY CHANGE HIS THINKING

WHEN INDOMITABLE SPIRIT FEELS LIKE HE DOES NOT FIT IN

HE SPEAKS WITH CONFIDENCE AND MAKES NEW FRIENDS

WHEN INDOMITABLE SPIRIT HAS FRIENDS WHO ARE A NEGATIVE INFLUENCE

HE STAYS TRUE TO HIMSELF AND NEVER LETS PEER PRESSURE BRING HIM DOWN A BAD PATH

WHEN TIMES ARE TOUGH AND THERE FEELS LIKE NO HOPE

INDOMITABLE SPIRIT ALWAYS SEES THE LIGHT AT THE END OF THE TUNNEL

AND FINDS A WAY TO STAY MOTIVATED AND TO KEEP GOING

HE NEVER ALLOWS FEELINGS OF DESPAIR AND HOPELESSNESS LET HIM FORGET THE REASONS HE IS NEEDED IN THIS WORLD

INDOMITABLE SPIRIT ALWAYS COMES OUT ON TOP BECAUSE HE NEEDS TO BE THERE FOR OTHERS TO HELP THEM WHEN THEY ARE LOST

IF YOU CAN ACT LIKE INDOMITABLE SPIRIT

YOU ARE ON THE WAY TO HAVING BLACK BELT CHARACTER TOO

NEXT TIME WE WILL MEET INDOMITABLE SPIRIT'S FRIENDS!